Nelson GRAMMAR

PUPIL BOOK 1

WENDY WREN

Nelson

Book 1 – Contents

This symbol shows that you need to correct mistakes in the text.

Nouns

Nouns are naming words.
They tell us the names of things.

cat　　　　　ball　　　　　fish　　　　　jug

Naming words are called **nouns**.

GRAMMAR *Focus*

Look at these pictures.
For each picture, choose the correct **noun** from the box. Write the nouns in your book.

hat

dog

peg

mug

man

bag

1 ＿＿＿＿＿＿　2 ＿＿＿＿＿＿　3 ＿＿＿＿＿＿

4 ＿＿＿＿＿＿　5 ＿＿＿＿＿＿　6 ＿＿＿＿＿＿

A Look around the room.
   Write the names of ten **nouns** you can see.

B Write the names of ten **nouns** you can see in this
   picture.

GRAMMAR *Extension*

Read this story.
Write the **nouns** in your book.

The girl was playing with her dog in the garden. The dog was running after a ball. The ball went under a bush. The dog went under the bush to find the ball.

Adjectives

Adjectives are describing words.
They tell us more about a person or thing.

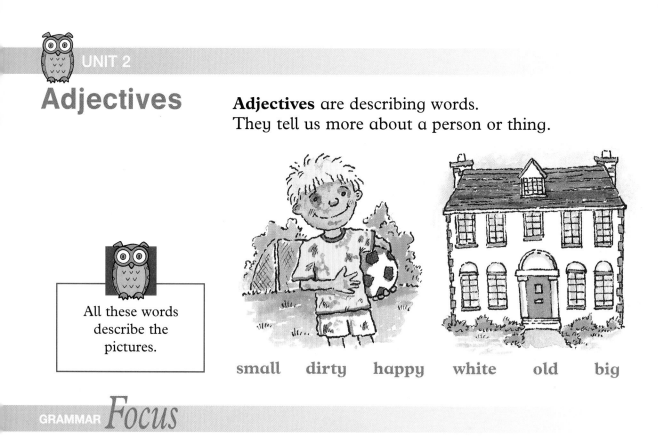

All these words describe the pictures.

small   dirty   happy   white   old   big

GRAMMAR *Focus*

Choose an **adjective** from the box for each animal.
Write the words in your book.

little
fluffy
brown
big
long
fat

1 _____   2 _____   3 _____

4 _____   5 _____   6 _____

Look at the picture.
Copy these sentences and fill in the missing **adjectives**.
You can use words from the box or adjectives of your own.

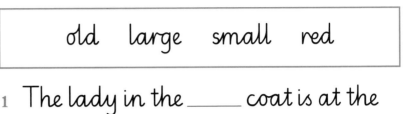

old   large   small   red

1 The lady in the ____ coat is at the bus stop.

2 The ____ boy is crying.

3 The ____ man has an umbrella.

4 On the roof there is a ____ cat.

GRAMMAR *Extension*

Read this story.
Write the **adjectives** in your book.

It was Ben's birthday. He wanted a blue bicycle with red handles. He had seen it in the new shop in town. He got some lovely cards and a big book of ghost stories. Mum and Dad had hidden the shiny bicycle in the shed. Ben was very happy when he saw the bicycle.

Singular and plural

Singular means 'one thing'.
Plural means 'more than one thing'.
We call one noun **singular**.
We call more than one noun **plural**.

If we are talking about more than one thing, we usually add an **s**.

A noun is a naming word.

one snail   two snail**s**   one monkey   two monkey**s**

GRAMMAR *Focus*

In your book, write these singular words as **plurals**.

1 three ball___   2 five hat___

3 two bat___   4 four tap___

A Look at the nouns in the box below.
Write a list of the nouns that are **singular**.
Now make a list of the nouns that are **plural**.

> sacks   ships   tree   logs
> cows   book   egg   coats
> fence   pens   mats

B Copy these sentences.
Underline the **plural** words.

1 The birds sat in the trees.

2 You need four eggs to make a cake.

3 Both cars were red.

4 My pens and pencils are in my
school bag.

GRAMMAR *Extension*

Copy this story.
Choose the correct word from each pair.

The old ship/ships was in the
river/rivers. It had two mast/masts
and a torn sail/sails. In one side/sides
there was a big hole/holes and the
water/waters was flooding in.

Prepositions

Prepositions are words which tell us where something is.

> A preposition tells us the position of something.

The cat is **on** the table.

The food is **in** the cat's mouth.

GRAMMAR *Focus*

Copy these sentences into your book.
Use a **preposition** from the box to fill each gap.

on

up

over

under

1
The woman is ____ the ladder.

2
The dog is ____ the table.

3
The cat is jumping ____ the wall.

4
The box is ____ the desk.

Look at these **prepositions**.

under   down   in   outside   on   over   off   up   out   inside

Write the pairs of **prepositions** which are opposites. One has been done for you.

under	over

Read this description and write down all the **prepositions** you can find.

The room was very neat and tidy.
The books were on the shelf and the newspapers were in the rack.
Under the table there was a red rug.
A picture hung over the fire and behind the door were pegs for coats.

Proper nouns

Nouns are the names of things

bush　　　　　　　　**girl**

Some nouns are special.

Chris is a special noun. It is someone's name.

Mr Black is a special noun. It is someone's name.

Special nouns are called **proper nouns**. Proper nouns start with a capital letter.

Your name is a proper noun.

GRAMMAR *Focus*

Copy these sentences into your book. Underline the **proper nouns**.

Mr King was going into town. He wanted to buy a book for his son Tom. He went into a book shop owned by Mr Williams. Mr King and Mr Williams were friends.

Look at the words in the box.
Find the **proper nouns**.

Copy the proper nouns into your book and
give each one a capital letter.

hat	fred	kim	duncan
tree	cat	mug	wendy
book	ali	meg	car

Copy these sentences into your book.
Use a **proper noun** to fill each gap.

1 My name is _____ _____.

2 My friend's name is _____ _____.

3 I would call a dog _____.

4 I would call a cat _____.

5 My mum's name is _____ _____.

6 My teacher's name is _____ _____.

Pronouns

A **pronoun** can be used instead of a noun.

The girl is running.
Girl is a **noun**.

She is running.
She is a **pronoun**.

The boy is reading.
Boy is a **noun**.

He is reading.
He is a **pronoun**.

It is a pronoun used for objects and animals.

GRAMMAR *Focus*

Some may have
more than one
pronoun.

Copy these sentences into your book.
Underline all the **pronouns**.

1 Where is he going?

2 He is going to the stream.

3 What has he found?

4 Where did he put it?

5 He has put it in the jar.

Practice

'They' is a useful pronoun for plural nouns.

Copy the sentences below.
Use **pronouns** from the box to replace the green words.

it	she	they

1 The little girl wanted an ice cream.
2 The elephant had a long trunk.
3 What are the boys playing?
4 Can you see the lion?

Extension

Look at this picture.

Write a sentence using a **pronoun** to answer each question.

1 What is the boy doing?
2 What is the girl doing?
3 What is the cat doing?
4 What is the dog doing?
5 What are the birds doing?

Confusing words

We often get the words **two** and **to** mixed up.

We use **two** like this:	We use **to** like this:
There are **two** birds	She is going **to** school.

GRAMMAR *Focus*

Copy these sentences into your book.
Fill the gaps with two or to.

1 There were _____ cakes left.

2 The stone sank _____ the bottom of the pond.

3 It is five minutes _____ six.

4 The _____ cups were broken.

5 We have playtime at _____ o'clock.

Remember to use capital letters and full stops.

A Use *two* or *to* to fill each gap.

1 I went ___ bed. 2 sixty-___

3 ___ pence 4 Jill ran ___ the park.

5 It is four days ___ Christmas.

B 1 Write your own sentence with the word *two* in it.
2 Write your own sentence with the word *to* in it.

GRAMMAR *Extension*

Copy this story.
Choose the correct word from each pair.

Sally was going two/to the shops.
She wanted two/to buy some bread
and two/to tins of soup. On the way
home she saw two/to of her friends.
Sally waved two/to her friends and
took the two/to tins of soup home.

17

Check-up 1

Nouns and adjectives

A In your book, write a list of the **nouns** you can see in this picture.

B Write an **adjective** to go with each noun in your list.

Plurals

A These words are singular.
Write the **plurals**.

1 car	2 stamp	3 hat
4 book	5 pen	6 pig
7 mat	8 road	9 shoe

B Use three of the **plurals** in sentences of your own.

Prepositions

Copy these sentences.
Fill each gap, using a **preposition** from the box.

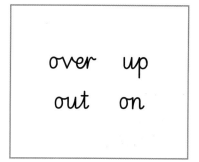

over   up

out   on

1 Sam is climbing _____ the stairs.

2 Rupa found the book _____ the shelf.

3 The cat jumped _____ the fence.

4 Raj took the dog _____ for a walk.

Proper nouns

Find the **proper nouns** in this box.
Write them with capital letters.

| tim lamb mrs desai frog |
| paul dan cap mr letts |

Pronouns

Copy these sentences.
Fill each gap with a **pronoun**.

1 Ian felt sick because _____ had eaten too much.

2 If Tina wanted, _____ could go to the match.

3 Aunt Mary was cross with the dog because _____ had chewed the rug.

Confusing words

Copy these sentences.
Fill each gap with two or to.

1 The sign pointed _____ the shops.

2 There were _____ socks on the washing line.

3 Which way do we go _____ get home?

4 The _____ bats were broken.

5 I have _____ leave in ten minutes.

Nouns

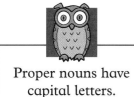

Proper nouns have capital letters.

Nouns are naming words.

hen   bicycle   table

The names of people are special nouns.
They are called **proper nouns**.

Mrs Flinn   Bill   Polly

Write these headings in your book.

nouns	proper nouns

Write each word from this box under the correct heading.

boot	Naseem	cart
Darren	Mr Evans	Mrs Patel
shark	horse	bowl
Harry	Mike	milk
cow	Tammy	Kamal

Copy these sentences.
Write the **proper nouns** with a capital letter

1 fred and kim were playing with a ball.

2 mr cap, the postman, was carrying letters.

3 rover, the dog, was chewing a bone.

4 julie ran across the field to meet nick.

5 mandy was not in school today.

Copy this story.
Fill in the gaps with **nouns** and **proper nouns** of your own.

Mr Knight was meeting his friend who was called ____ ____.
He put on his ____ and ____ and went out. Mrs ____ was in her ____ and she waved to Mr ____.
He closed the ____, waved to ____ ____ and went to meet ____ ____.

21

Adjectives

Adjectives are describing words.
They tell us more about nouns.

Nouns are
naming words.

adjective   thin
noun   man

adjective   angry
noun   tiger

GRAMMAR *Focus*

In your book, write an **adjective** and a **noun** for
each picture.

1 _____ 2 _____ 3 _____ 4 _____

5 _____ 6 _____ 7 _____ 8 _____

Write ten **adjectives** to describe this robot.

GRAMMAR *Extension*

This story has no adjectives.
Copy the story into your book but add **adjectives** as you go along to make it more interesting.

The farmer was working in the field. He was wearing a coat, a scarf and a hat. On his feet he wore boots. He drove the tractor up and down the field, making furrows so that he could plant the seed which would grow into corn.

Simple sentences

A **sentence** tells us something.
It make sense.

This is a sentence:

> **The clouds in the sky are grey.**

This is not a sentence:

> **the large grey clouds**

A sentence begins with a **capital letter** and ends with a **full stop**.

A sentence has to make sense.

GRAMMAR *Focus*

Copy these **sentences** into your book.
Begin each sentence with a **capital letter** and end it with a **full stop**.

1 the bus was late

2 the broken glass was thrown away

3 it rained all day

4 the lion slept in the sun

5 the birds made their nests in the tree

6 in winter it is very cold

After

two

cats

Flowers

Today

Fill the gaps to make each of these a **sentence**.
The words in the box will help you.

1 _____ begin to grow in the spring.

2 Dogs like to chase _____.

3 _____ tea, we went out to play.

4 Bicycles usually have _____ wheels.

5 _____ is my birthday.

GRAMMAR *Extension*

Look for the capital letters and full stops to help you.

Write the words in the correct order to make **sentences**.

1 man driving The was car. his

2 are the in There flowers vase.

3 The on table. was food the

Copy these **verb** webs.
Use the words in the box to complete the webs.

| howls | | pours | |

trickles
barks
chases
patters

A Copy these sentences.
Choose a **verb** of your own to fill each gap.

1 I like _____ sand castles on the beach.

2 The snow is _____ very quickly.

3 I _____ for eight hours each night.

4 We _____ outside in the summer.

5 I like _____ my story book.

B Use these verbs in sentences of your own.

1 digging   2 falling   3 painting

Questions

Some sentences **tell** us something.
Some sentences **ask** us something.
Telling sentences end with a full stop.

The duck is on the pond.

Asking sentences are called **questions**.
They end with a question mark.

Try writing a few
question marks.

What is the time?

GRAMMAR *Focus*

Which of these are **questions**?
Copy the questions into your book.

1 I looked at the moon last night.

2 Did you see the moon?

3 What time did you go to bed?

4 It was cold this morning.

5 Did it snow last night?

6 Have you got your coat?

Copy these sentences.
End each one with a **full stop** or a **question mark**.

1 Can you tell me where the shops are

2 Is it raining

3 The bicycle is in the shed

4 I like drawing

5 Do you like playing football

6 Where have you put my pen

GRAMMAR *Extension*

Remember your question marks.

A Write a **question** to go with each of these answers.

1 It is ten o'clock.

2 I had beans on toast for tea.

3 I have left my book at home.

4 I like chocolate very much.

5 I hurt my arm when I fell over.

6 My Mum is over there.

B Write down three **questions** to ask a friend.

Verbs

A **verb** is a doing or 'active' word.

A verb tells us what is being done in a sentence.

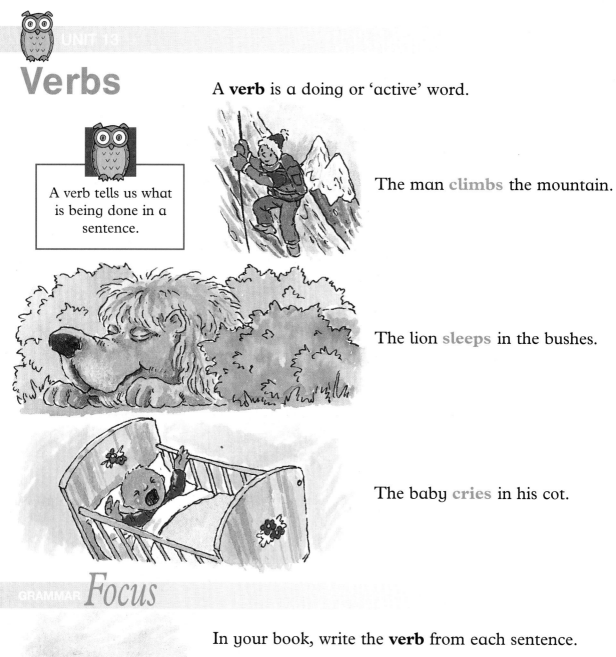

The man **climbs** the mountain.

The lion **sleeps** in the bushes.

The baby **cries** in his cot.

GRAMMAR *Focus*

In your book, write the **verb** from each sentence.

1 Carol plays the piano very well.

2 The children read to their teacher.

3 The farmer plants the seed.

4 The river flows down the hill.

5 The wood burns on the bonfire.

Copy these sentences.
Choose the best **verb** for each sentence.

1 We _____ into the swimming pool.

| hop | dive | throw |

2 Birds _____ from tree to tree.

| run | fly | swing |

3 The dog _____ his bone.

| paints | drinks | chews |

GRAMMAR *Extension*

Remember your
capital letters and
full stops.

Write a sentence to say what is happening in
each picture. Underline the **verbs**.

Check-up 2

Nouns

Look around the room.
Write a list of five **nouns** that you can see.
Write a list of five **proper nouns**.

Nouns and adjectives

A Write these headings in your book.

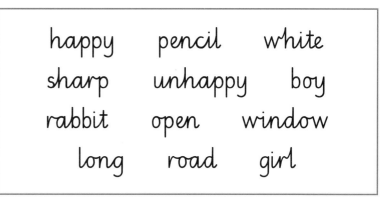

noun	adjective

Write each word from this box under the correct heading.

happy	pencil	white
sharp	unhappy	boy
rabbit	open	window
long	road	girl

B Match each of the **adjectives** from your list with one of the **nouns**.
Write the pairs in your book.

Simple sentences

A Make these into **sentences** by using **capital letters** and **full stops**.

1 the children worked hard

2 the spider spun a web

3 we went out when the rain stopped

4 after tea I played a game

5 on Saturdays we go shopping

B Put the words in order to make **sentences**.

1 was The hungry. cat

2 white. is house My

3 the Put light on.

Verbs

A Copy these sentences.
Underline the **verbs**.

1 The teacher talks to the class.

2 The girl sings loudly.

3 My dad wakes up early.

4 You eat toast every morning.

B Use these **verbs** in sentences of your own.

1 washing 2 carrying 3 singing

Questions

A Copy these sentences.
End each one with a **full stop** or a **question mark**.

1 May I have that

2 Am I in time for the bus

3 The truck has a flat tyre

4 My window is broken

5 Is that my book

B Write a **question** to go with each answer.

1 I have been in the playground.

2 Two and two make four.

3 I am going upstairs.

Adjectives

Adjectives are describing words.
Adjectives describe nouns.

adjective	angry	**adjective**	unhappy
noun	man	**noun**	clown

Colours are adjectives.
They tell us the colour of nouns.

 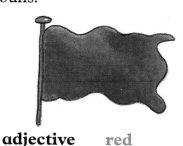

adjective	blue	**adjective**	red
noun	car	**noun**	flag

GRAMMAR *Focus*

Match an **adjective** from the box with each noun.
Write the pairs in your book.

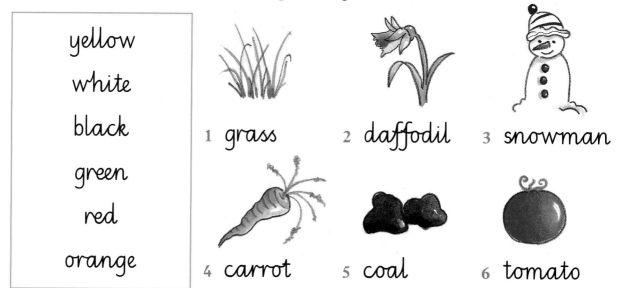

| yellow |
| white |
| black |
| green |
| red |
| orange |

1 grass   2 daffodil   3 snowman

4 carrot   5 coal   6 tomato

Copy these sentences.
Fill in the gaps with **colour adjectives** of your own.

1 The _____ berries on the bush were eaten by the _____ birds.

2 The _____ bananas and the _____ apples are in the bowl.

3 The children played in the _____ sea and on the _____ sand.

4 The grapes are _____ and _____ .

GRAMMAR *Extension*

Write five sentences about this picture.
Use a **colour adjective** in each sentence.

Conjunctions

Conjunctions are words we use to join sentences. The conjunction we use most is **and**.

When you make one sentence, you only need one capital letter and one full stop.

Sentence 1:
Mary picked an apple.

Sentence 2:
She ate it.

We can use **and** to join the two sentences:

Mary picked an apple **and** she ate it.

GRAMMAR *Focus*

Use *and* to join these pairs of sentences.
Write them in your book

1 The cat ran after the bird.
  It flew away.

2 It rained all night.
  The road was flooded.

3 The boy threw a stone.
  The window was broken.

4 The day was very hot.
  We went for a swim.

Pronouns are 'he, she, it, they'.

A Copy these sentences.
Change the red words into **pronouns**.

1 Sarah went to the shop.
Sarah bought some apples.

2 Jim found a glove in the playground. Jim took it to school.

3 The children forgot their bags.
The children were late for school.

4 The mouse saw the cat.
The mouse ran into a hole.

B Join each pair of sentences from part A with *and*.

GRAMMAR *Extension*

A Write two short sentences about each picture.

Remember, one capital letter and one full stop for each sentence.

1

2

3

4

B Join each pair of sentences from part A with *and*.

Verbs

Verbs are doing words or 'active' words.

Tammy **walks** quickly.

Walks tells us what Tammy does.
Verbs can be put into families.
The name of a verb family starts with **to**.

Family name	Verbs in the family
to walk	walk walks walking walked
to play	play plays playing played

Grammar *Focus*

Write these **verb family names** in your book.

to look	to jump	to brush

Write each **verb** from the box under the correct family name.

brushed   looked   jumps
looking   jumped
brushed   jumping   brushes

Practice

Copy these sentences.
Choose the right **verb** to finish each sentence.

1 Jim is run/running in a race.

2 Is your dad fish/fishing today?

3 We go/going to the shops every Saturday.

4 I am try/trying my best.

5 Did you put/putting the box on the table?

Extension

A Write three **verbs** to go with each of these verb families.

1 to leap	2 to bang
3 to talk	4 to paint
5 to pray	6 to cook
7 to wish	8 to scratch

B Write the family names of these **verbs**.

1 counted	2 catches
3 drops	4 finding
5 shouted	6 sweeps

Pronouns

A noun is a
naming word.

A pronoun can be used instead of a noun.

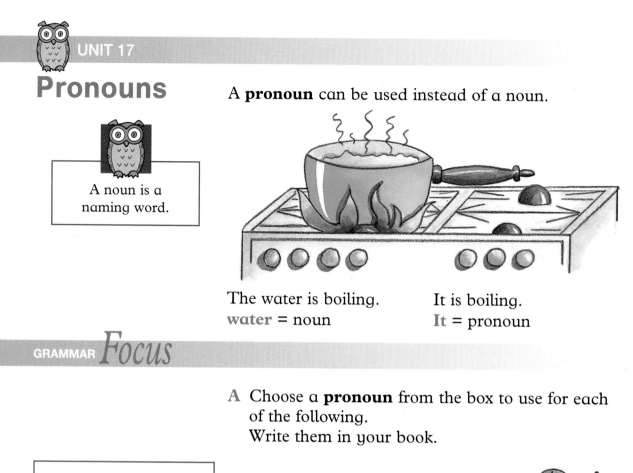

The water is boiling.
water = noun

It is boiling.
It = pronoun

GRAMMAR *Focus*

A Choose a **pronoun** from the box to use for each
of the following.
Write them in your book.

he
she
it
they

1 _____ 2 _____ 3 _____

4 _____ 5 _____ 6 _____

B What **pronoun** would you use instead of your
own name?

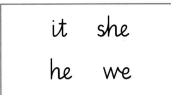

it   she

he   we

Copy these sentences.
Use **pronouns** from the box to replace the green words.

1 John and I stayed after school so that John and I could watch the match.

2 Dinesh saved his pocket money so that Dinesh could buy a book.

3 The puppy chewed the shoe and Dad was cross with the puppy.

4 When Lisa had a cold, Lisa did not go to school.

GRAMMAR *Extension*

Finish these sentences so that each one has a different **pronoun**.

1 The rain _____.

2 One day _____.

3 After school _____.

4 If it is sunny tomorrow _____.

5 The girl _____.

41

Adjectives

Nouns are naming words.

Adjectives are describing words.
They describe nouns.

Adjectives can describe the size of a noun.

fat cat   **small** mouse

Adjectives can describe the colour of a noun.

green book   **yellow** flower

Adjectives can describe the number of nouns.

two cups   **ten** bricks

GRAMMAR *Focus*

In your book, write the **number adjective** to go with each of these nouns.

1 _____ gloves   2 _____ shells   3 _____ ants   4 _____ cakes

Practice

Copy the sentences below.
Underline the **number adjective** in blue.
Underline the **colour adjective** in red.

1 I saw five white swans on the lake.

2 There are seven blue cups on the shelf.

3 Will you buy six red apples?

4 I need three black buttons.

5 Ten green bottles were standing on the wall.

Extension

Look at this picture.

Write some sentences to describe the picture.
Use at least three **number adjectives** and three **colour adjectives**.

Conjunctions

Conjunctions are words we use to join sentences.

The conjunction we use most is **and**.
Give me the rubbish.   I will take it outside.
Give me the rubbish **and** I will take it outside.

Another conjunction we often use is **but**.
The telephone rang.   No one answered it.
The telephone rang **but** no one answered it.

GRAMMAR *Focus*

Use but to join each pair of sentences to make one sentence. Write the sentences in your book.

1 One of our players was hurt.
  We won the match.

2 I wanted a plum.
  There were none left.

3 It rained a lot today.
  Josh went out to play.

4 The car crashed into the tree.
  The driver was not hurt.

5 I have to go to the dentist.
  I do not want to.

A Copy these sentences.
Change the red words into **pronouns**.

1 Fred could not get to sleep.
Fred was not tired the next day.

2 Sean likes oranges. Sean does not want one now.

3 The birds built a nest. The birds did not lay any eggs.

4 My friend and I missed the train. My friend and I got there on time.

B Use but to join each pair of sentences that you made in Part A.

GRAMMAR *Extension*

Use and or but to join these pairs of sentences.

1 I have lost the book. I need it.

2 Mike forgot his lunchbox. He was very hungry when he got home.

3 It was a very cold day.
My new coat kept me warm.

4 Naseem likes drawing.
He does not like painting.

Check-up 3

Nouns

A 1 Write three **nouns** beginning with the letter 's'.

2 Write three **nouns** beginning with the letter 'p'.

B Copy these sentences.
Write the **proper nouns** with capital letters.

1 mrs lock and amy have red coats.

2 My friend is called jabbar.

3 If they break the glass, harry and donna will be in trouble.

Adjectives

A Copy these sentences and fill the gaps with **adjectives**.

1 The _____ dog ran around the _____ garden.

2 Please find a _____ box for these _____ clothes.

B Copy these sentences and use a **colour adjective** to finish each one.

1 The _____ sunset was beautiful.

2 I have a _____ watch.

3 Steve wanted a _____ dog.

C Copy these sentences and complete each one with a **number adjective**.

1 There are _____ days in a week.

2 There are _____ weeks in a year.

3 There are _____ months in a year.

Nouns and adjectives

Write the headings *noun* and *adjective*.
Write the words in this box under the correct headings.

cold jug red man purple bag
three table big boot rain

Plurals

Choose the correct word to complete each sentence.

1 There is one comic/comics left.
2 I have two pound/pounds in my purse.
3 There were ten ticket/tickets left to sell.

Prepositions

Write a sentence using each of these **prepositions**.

1 under   2 down   3 inside
4 out   5 in   6 over

Pronouns

Copy these sentences, changing the blue words into **pronouns**.

1 Have you found the key?
2 Mum and I like ice cream.
3 The boys went to the park.
4 The old man walked with a stick.

47

Confusing words

Choose the correct word to complete each sentence.

1 I have to/two days to finish this work.

2 It is time to/two go out.

Simple sentences

A Put the words in the right order to make **sentences**.

1 fire. on The was house

2 go have out. I to

B Finish each sentence with a **full stop** or a **question mark**.

1 How are you today

2 My hand hurts

Conjunctions

Join each pair of sentences using *and* or *but*.

1 You can play in the snow. You must put on your coat.

2 The bird pecked at the ground. It found a worm.

Verbs

A Fill each gap with a **verb**.

1 Liz _____ the book.

2 The badger _____ into its hole.

B Write the **family name** of each **verb**.

1 talking   2 crying   3 makes

C Write two **verbs** to go with each **family name**.

1 to grow   2 to clean   3 to laugh

48